All Our Wonder Unavenged

All Our Wonder Unavenged

Don Domanski

Brick Books

Library and Archives Canada Cataloguing in Publication

Domanski, Don, 1950-
    All our wonder unavenged / Don Domanski.

Poems.
ISBN-13: 978-1-894078-58-0
ISBN-10: 1-894078-58-6.

I. Title.

PS8557.O43A64 2007   C811'.54   C2006-906534-9

We acknowledge the Canada Council for the Arts, the Government of
Canada through the Book Publishing Industry Development Program
(BPIDP), and the Ontario Arts Council for their support of our publishing
program.

Cover art, "Gateway", 2005, 6 in. x 7 in., pen and ink on paper,
by Don Domanski.

The author photograph was taken by Jie Sun.

The book is set in Minion and News Gothic.

Design and layout by Alan Siu.

Brick Books
431 Boler Road, Box 20081
London, Ontario N6K 4G6

www.brickbooks.ca

for Mary

Names are only the guests of reality.
~ Hsu Yu

Contents

In the Dream of the Yellow Birches

Drowning Water

Leaning on Silk

1.

an October morning after another sleepless night
I lift the window to let in the little strengths of the day

all night the house felt like it was underwater
red gills beneath each shingle opening and closing
                                        to receive the air

now the view from the window is waterless   dry grass
and bright sky with a few crows hitched to maples

the sun is out of plain sight   over there near the edges
of salvation   bringing the bees to life   autumn coming
down after dark to lie awhile upon the earth

no freeze yet to switch off hearts and turn up the elegies
no frost yet to escort the mould beneath the ferns

just quietude now and eyelids of soil lowered over granite
and roads collecting dead leaves   the little sweep along
of the breeze   redness of leaves like coal fires
starting to catch   the Carboniferous blush
                                 that keeps saying good-bye.

2.

almost 8 a.m. and cars are scurrying beneath the leaves
reminding me of Egyptian scarabs   dorbeetles coppery-gold
and dog-blue and green as two landscapes
superimposed one upon the other   the way day is made

I drink coffee while looking out the window
warmth of a star standing with me in the kitchen
the house breathing softly against my ear   the dead fly
on the counter resembling another house far away
a dark house that I almost remember   where I'm certain
some secret still lies   its bones set to low music
like water over stones   its skin petalled with lost sleep

amen to secrets   to all these mornings hidden beneath
sunlight   where the heavens can never find us
our small secrets holding us to the earth   rituals
and fetishes mothering us on through storm and silence
our mantra in the bedroom just before we wake
later the coffee's prayer steaming up   gliding by
indistinguishable from our minds pushed high
                                                    into the ether
the edges of vacancy lingering there   thought and concept
uncombed   vapour into vapour   trailing away.

3.

last night I watched the stars and once-stars   infinity
on the quiet   sliding over the trees   flames entrusted
to expectancy   to the next moment   the next secret
all those bottomless fires flashed across space   hiding
countless worlds with light   all those endless solitudes
sealed in shine   ungetable in the glare   ecstasy
sunstruck into the hush of things   slow burn of séance
into séance   solar heat stung into rock and flesh
chemical ghosts curled clockwise   asleep in the tan

I stood for an hour or so watching the welkin nose west
reclusive lustre of the infinite pushing itself along
on one edgeless shadow   no overseer plying embraces
bosoming in the welts of light   not a machine either
but the heat of an absent god   his slow turn away
                                        from the margins

I stood feeling that absence   because we are born to it
because the night sky is part of our nervous system
stellar scends luminous   softly bright along neural pathways
a celestial glow seeping into blood   the vault of heaven
in every cell like breath blown clear of the body
tumble of flames in each gesture we make
everywhere a radiancy lit by our movements   our frowns
                                our small walks across the earth.

4.

I'm watching each direction add up the sunlight
making a day of it   another Monday among the sticks
and milkweed   bees' blood in the air   cats walking
offstage   bare places calling in their children

morning grunges on beneath varying skies
in any other life I would still be standing here
witnessing the high camouflage of blue air
hearing at every moment the low thrum of the ego
that eerie enchantment with naming the self

in any other life I would still wait with the gravel
for the frost to come silvering in   the stars
would still hold their Newtonian dissolve
their slow lapse behind time

slouching and half-asleep at the window   I lean on
a memory of stars which is like leaning on silk
the folds of it collapsing into self-regard
that secretive pride in loving what can't be owned

but that pride fades   it always does   sinks
like the thin clasp of serenity fastened onto water
our egos *writ on water* so pitiful in morning's glitter.

5.

a few dark clouds are coming in from the northwest
later the writings of rain on all the roads out of the city
doctrines on quietism and impermanence   precepts
that influence one person out of a million   that person
indistinguishable from the water falling
from the trees holding their breath against their sides

a codling moth is fluttering against the window pane
some are still alive in October   a few of those drifting
                          off each night with the wrong angel

a few of us too   sliding into shadows   becoming
a bit of dust on the agony tree or a gaze fallen
or the gloam bladed thin among the idols of grass

we vanish the way the bright edges of water vanish
silently like the heart's cipher   the way the body
                          makes its chemistry without names

the moth has settled against the glass   stilled
deeper into the moment by the great holding of itself

thin strip of wings shivered into place
this is where the night will gather   stars over cities
moon rising   lovers afoot in whisper's gravity

when I look closely I can see it has a pattern
of interlacing fingers along its body
it holds me beneath them when I'm sleeping

I'm exhausted and leaning on the kitchen counter

the moth has settled against the glass
its mind is a pair of wings trembling
its mind is like that sensation of falling
just a moment before sleep.

Our Little Boat Drifting

a blindness along the surface of the water
the dead seeing there in the dark

our little boat drifting
our eyes shut   our mouths closed
we will try together to never open them again

the stars are paintings on walls
but the walls are very far away
and all the lands of the earth
are very far away

beneath us the living are water
                    the dead are salt
and although we've tried all night
although we've tried for countless nights
we can't tell one from the other
we can't separate them with our longing.

Leviathan

(New Victoria, Cape Breton)
            for Tim Bowling

1.

I was twelve and all the waves
were growing old growing moonward
under my great-uncle's boat
and like all children
I could hear the voice
within each drop of water
each an oath to the other   a vow
each to the destiny of the other
holding us firmly among them
their efforts blue with labour
labouring the globe to a promise
far beneath us where new feelings
new names rose up out of the depths
I spent a summer on that boat
almost anonymous among relatives
men I hardly knew   watching them drag
each grey complexion day after day
out of the sea's glistening face
I saw how they closed their eyes
when they hauled cod onto the boat
how their shadows reached more
into the effort than their bodies
I saw how they released those shadows
when we came ashore
allowing them to drift along the ground
to find openings
crevices to slide into

between perdition and the thistle's root
shadows gone so they could be
apart from Death and Death's flesh
the fine filigree woven like netting
that crossed over and under
the closing of each day.

2.

every evening my great-aunt would saw off
the heads of cod
with a large serrated knife
reminding me of the magician's coffin
where before going to bed each night
the story went he sawed his bride in two
his eros complete
in the movement of the blade

my cousin would gut them one by one
the offal being all the loose knots
that held each soul in place
a fishy soul full of inwardness
the star's blindness
the sea's trace on silence

that bucket of offal was the most
ancient of fables
in there the witch ate her children
the ogre returned home to find the intruder
the worm found an eye alone in the grass

in there wars   corpses on the ground
whoring for heartbeats among the ferns
the trooper's ghost drawn
with a few strokes of blood in the air

in there the seven cities of Troy
whispering among themselves
inventing the hero
his ire the colour of a crow's blush
his pride the colour of petals
chasing after the earth.

3.

later when we had gone upstairs
and put out the lights
I would lie in my bed listening
and all the fish in the ocean were still
and the stillness stretched itself
over something that had been empty forever
and from under that emptiness Leviathan
would come each night to swallow us
because slumber is the judgement of the sea
because unconsciousness is the severity
of that judgement   unknowingness
its penalty   its retribution and sting
and while being swallowed we would each mouth
our name like hake trying to breathe on dry land
we would touch our blood with closed eyes

and forget sight   forget ever having been awake
we would lie back embracing in sleep
a mouldering of the mind's absence
the god we prayed to   that terrible angel
that splash of darkness under each and every stone.

Five Thousand Young Deer

grey day in Halifax   harbour calm
the morning soluble in water
rain falling on the hour's back
                which tightens with light

I stand at the edge of the pier   the sea
is breathing in its own body   the undertow
like five thousand young deer drawing back
                    from a hunter's memory
from the force of daybreak falling upon the waves.

Slayer in a Told World

the shadows of rabbits sleep among hounds
snow falls   calling in its light from the hills

underfoot the road passes the darkness along
while all the lower worlds climb to higher ground

overhead clouds continue their single thought
which is accessible to everyone but them
they think of a deity   a phase transition
sweet as evaporation   cool as mist

the God of Clouds drifting through the forest
bearded in the movements of deer
ever-returning to the edges of things

I walk feeling the weight of snow above me
the untranslatable whispered off like vapour
the nudge of extinction   clench of nativity
a knowledge lost in signatures
in the signing of cells throughout the body

we are lonely for whatever abides
in the calluses of ice on bark
and among roots thrown carelessly beneath trees
a weathering of gods against the trunks
withstanding supplications   all the night's prayers
the ending of prospects   where the solitude goes

we long for falling snow   its iconography
enshrined at the velocity of instinct
just within sight   outstretched and taken
to its weight at the horizon

each flake standing for the myriad things
that live well beyond our language
silence of the animal mind descending
that longevity   that slayer in a told world.

An Old Animal Habit

nothing much to attend the stars tonight
small talk of the weeds   koan of a boulder
a line of trees in angelic orders   the dead
remembering all those candles they once lit
                        in the sleeping woods

this world can only be as large as a pond's contentment
no larger   cool water lined with stones and grass
unmown grass Lethean green under the street lights
blades casting the shadows of eternity's alphabet
small Aramaic strokes of darkness on parched ground

I walk along like blood seeking its wound
an old animal habit   attentiveness to movement
backwash of my body trailing narratives behind me
stories like cut fingers on someone else's hand

there are roots under my feet   scaffolds packed in soil
where dark ages hang filling their throats with water
there are nightjars above me   calling to their masters
to those forces vague and unseeable
infolded with clouds somewhere high above the city

I'm on Willow Street again   the earth one step
                        ahead of me in the dark
a fog moving in from the harbour
a slight breeze like butterflies pulling the plow of Eros
the street like a greenhouse drifting gradually out to sea

the mind's amorphous shape in each footstep   a pain
in my lower back   synaptic bitch-work of the body
effigies of roses set on fire between my vertebrae
red flowers vamping up   lit and bladed through

each of my thoughts like the ghost of a key trying
                                        to turn in a lock
to let in the imagined self   that story in the bloodstream
veined like a long pause   its fadeout to edgeless space

nowhere to write down what I love   what loves me
only the missing words adrift among the chestnut leaves
only a wordless prayer   lip-sync of the black water
                            pooling behind our bright eyes

nowhere to turn where there isn't a brushstroke or two
of absence shining through   catching the light
                            we give to things

nowhere to place the heart   some grace found between
the beats   a feather's dharma turning over in my chest
weight of the soul before any decision is made
afterwards a hawk's quill to write it all down
                            the sigh and apocalypse.

Fledge

days and nights assimilated into the foliage
Year of the Sea Change or just about

sunlight hot and unappeasable
the honey ill   the salt out of breath

neighbourhood dogs sheathing human
voices with their own   wasps casting
the shadows of crumbs falling from a table

stones balanced in their one footstep

no one coming to visit   no names to remember
a reclusive repose among the brawn of dragonflies

I sit in the shade all day and at night the stars
                                    are like krill in the air

I sit beside the loosestrife signalling back from
their listening posts   blossoms in their sixth sense
intuition steady and weightless in their stems

I watch time ever-returning to its old address
under the scar of crows on the gingko tree
some part of each hour sewn up in fledge   winged
and battle-dark along the loosening cosmologies
that separate sky and earth   thunder and fireweed

some part of ourselves taken aside   given charity
and flight   although you wouldn't know it to look
at us   our pose unlikely to carry us anywhere
unfeathered and lodged in the slightness of hands

sleeves of a species   diaphanous and shyly laced
in our affections   in our slip away to the roses
small traces of us left in the endings and half-truths

our flyovers paling out like water in the eye
like an absence screen-tested twice along the hedges

our low glides staining our hearts the colour
of pigeons roosting at twilight on a ledge
the blur of their wings landing is the colour I mean
the spirit in the motion just beyond their descent.

Drowning Water

1.

the cormorant carries the universe
it's a place small enough for a bird to carry

on its back the countryside tilts down to the sea
beneath its feathers a well runs deeply down into its body

you haul water up in a tin bucket
the water isn't red like cormorant's blood
but clear like the skill of drinking from your palms
folded   holding an invisible cup   you drink the cup
and unfold your hands reaching for the water again.

2.

you take the water indoors   it enters a room trembling
it enters a house afraid even though it's been there before
even though it's been in the belly of a whale   in a teapot
in the eyes of Seneca   in a shot glass   in a glacier
even though it's passed through sewers and aquariums
been under Phoenician ships and in the stems of roses
in the wings of locusts rising from a decision in the dark

it enters the house shivering as if it were cold
even though it has been mixed with blood   with soup
with earth   with food dyes that have made it bluer
than blue ever wanted to be   even though Lao-Tzu
slept with it beneath his tongue   calling it a flame
even though it has rested in the warmth of
countless breasts   awaiting the child foretold by emptiness
although each time the infant is only water and morning
the ocean come back from death   laying down its head.

3.

at every moment water is finished with itself   complete
with memories   with motion   with resting-places
but because of you it begins again to move the hours
into position   it picks you up once again from sleep

all day it will protect you from thirst   which is the voice
of the enemy in your throat longing to speak   to curse
the wisdom of the elements   the raindrop's preeminence
over humanity   the rapture in the plumbing
ecstasy in the kettle   the exaltation in the cloud

you who are so graceless   drowning water with your gestures
understand its patience   its tender stillness in a bowl
its true life is a silence that is always present
the faraway in an animal's mouth   the dowry of a bride unborn

you who are so unconscious   so wet with thought   know
when you leave it will wait for you   wait years for you
to return   then it will be a name to remember when you open
the door   water   a name for your name to return to.

Mere

I lie beside a pond   hidden by weeds
the nearest things are approaching
a hush is like a place
shining water and shining stones
homecoming is an ever-receding will
then a breeze outstretched to clouds
then a sparrow carried on a stranger's wings.

Water Strider

the pond is ectoplasm   I walk on ghosts
apparitional gatherings carry me along
spook quilted to spook quilted to hunger
and the sighs of glassworts to lead me
I am mothered by phantoms everlasting
I am fathered by a rocking distance
beneath and above the water

my body sheds its strides behind me
I am coir-headed with thatched eyes
with mandibles deposited at the corners of light

I put myself through margins
slide across my own jumps
the film under me covers a shadow
as calm as a hunter risen to flesh

I glide reaches to mosquito larvae
I feed and return to voracity

skidding along wraiths I come to no end
nothing teaches me more than once
all doctrine is edible   digestible
whatever pain I feel is less than failure
all death is incomprehensible
all hurt draws a luminosity
all wounds close as night comes.

Untitled with Invisible Ink

I know a wood where each leaf is the distance between two dark towns, where each branch contains what is granted to kingdoms and I know the wind that carries all of that away. I know a tree in that wood and a stone in that wood, because we have sat for long hours and together we have the energy of a shaken man, the energy I wouldn't have, seated just by myself. I know a house at the edge of that wood, a small house with a woman whose heart is saddened in slow motion, broken in places the blood doesn't know. I've heard her weeping through the crickets and the vetch, because they carry what is hidden out into the world. I've heard the sound of silk in her throat when she struggles for words, and the sound of firelight spreading across water when she's sleeping. I've seen her up close and I've seen her far away, and I've seen her hands adjust that distance with a motion. She wrote this small poem in her small house, but she doesn't know. She wrote it with whatever is akin to breathing, sighs and breath against the panes, the fog that rolls out of that original ocean fathoms down in the body. I know those waters, the covering waves, the fish that carry the language through. We come from there with our words and our deeds, all the fin-trailings of what is left unspoken. The light down there is like a small house lit by a candle, just enough brightness to read by, to write by with invisible ink, enough glow to allow for the soul to go further than the fingertips, to bend over the answers and hesitate, and to pick up the pen which isn't there.

Twa Corbies

winter half awake on spruce boughs

clouds sewn poorly onto the sky

two dead crows lying in the snow
each body a trunk full of God's dark clothes
to be worn on the Day of Judgement
on that day of the smaller catechisms
     the feathered ones

I've been walking through the stand-down
of light along the river dusk another disguise
for the utterances sleep-talking of what's calling
to us at the close of each day

the storyline of trees darkening down into a poem
by Anon the one about *twa corbies*
the newly-slain knight lying beneath his shield
shield like a door pressing into a small room
where the medicine is kept the bandages stored
     in a deep measure of psalms

a murder of crows just now scrolling along
the branches of an oak reading aloud from
     their Book of Hours
inlay of black words gleaming up black pages
into black books that snap their covers shut
and fly away

simple enough to dismiss their screed   their vows
rabbiting on and on into cold air
simple enough to miss the message   *The the*
as Stevens wrote awhile ago in Hartford

easy to lose our way   fall back to a downsize
of the possible   surrender to attainment

easy to believe our lips whiten the edges of darkness
when we speak of darkness   easy to fool ourselves
to shepherd the infinite till each day is done
                              and scored with fire

Tuesday evening coming up slowly now between the hills
already preening itself along the eastern horizon
grey and wordless   wordless and immortal
no second thoughts in its ascension   nothing rehearsed

it'll carry me home   breath and all

I'll just wait for it here beside the unceasing guise
of the river   water bowing to water   shine to shine
everlasting in its destinations

a few flakes of snow are falling   time going through the trees
from one heart to another   behind my back *twa corbies* rolling
up their wounds   calling it quits   flying home once more
                              through the welkin.

The Feather

for Robert Weaver

six hundred miles of trees
nine hundred miles of rain

tonight the progeny
of grass are born behind
all the faces that sleep

tonight the thin ankles
of the porcupine glow
with the light of asylums

tonight Rome and all the Caesars
are finally enclosed in the folds
of the moth's wing

tonight the logging road breathes
evenly under my feet   I reach down
touch the hem of a harrier feather

it rises slowly from the ground
moves steadily off into space

it'll find the god of hawks
nesting in the dark reach
of all ascension

it'll rest in motion

it'll disappear before we wake.

Walking Down to Acheron

1.

I walk along a road leading down to the river
underfoot hieroglyphs from the Devonian Age
sealed tightly in flat grey stones   overhead
clouds ease back from the horizon   into one
continuous shadow of Destiny's resolve

a cool day in June   house finches handing out the sky
the earth lying like a grain of wheat in a great barn
                    the moon whispering under straw

a light drizzle keeping time with the pollen
coyotes wandering the hills   God in their legs

how quietly the senses move between the pine trees
like vapour through the needling of light.

2.

I remember last summer finding a pond near here
spending an afternoon watching dragonflies hover
their every heartbeat fastened with pins
one to the next to the final one outside the world

I knelt down and touched the water   barely
like an old appointment scarcely kept   the surface
pulse of the pool pushing back against my fingers
which I knew was you   dead and set to music
you in a hymn darkly spread   away and placeless

I recalled that part of the Heart Sutra where it says
The infinitely far away is not only near, but it's infinitely

near. It's nowhere, and nowhere it is not. I was certain
I could live with that   just that and the tension of water
                                        against my fingertips.

3.

today there's the walk to the river   rounded corners
of the phantasmal   the shifting plurality of matter
rocks and trees   the brassy oaths of grackles
the subsoil underslung with the respiration
of Heaven   foxes with amulets ribbing their physiques
luck of spring and full bellies   and my small ghost
making its way through
                    continuously emptying flesh into breath

today there's my shadow on the summits of dandelions
on damp weeds   on the figureheads of stumps
there's the ache that goes before me   wraithing
around turns in the path   that desire for deliverance
the soul's nudge   that little jinx in the body

a good idea to ignore it   to look the other way
watch granite boulders dog-eared in the earth
count the trees   the fallen ones   about to fall still
further into Acheron and be carried away like mist
acknowledge the tamarack clotted into flower
the plantain   all the grasses of no fixed address

notice the sun's appearance over the treetops
over each darkness turning in its resting place
over the far-off sound of the river maffling
like the voices of the ancients sealed in hives
open-mouthed   a fathom down in the honey.

4.

a good time of day to attend to all the details
keep an eye on the clouds holding their great fires
notice the days curled up in the tracks of deer
watch a pair of mourning doves walk back and forth
along the banks of the river   like two lame girls
stopping at intervals to circle the absence of a third

it's that third dove the soul is always seeking
some part of us always looking for what can't be seen
                         what won't be revealed

I'll take comfort in the river coursing along its stones
flowing east through its fetishes   faded embraces
miming connections at the eddies   doubling back
on themselves like thought   every vortex thinking clear
as bright water   speeds polished by atom-fall through
the crossings   their circuits of pure light

I'll console myself with the flowering-rush growing
along the shoreline   with its rhizomes in deep nativity
with speckled trout steadying themselves in the current
each fin a hunch that the world is still there
each move of their tails a doubt   a push of suspicion

I'll take solace now in this snail intersecting my path
its horns pressing into the solitude of God   just there
where it hurts   where grief begins.

5

I'll sit here with slender kingdoms for awhile
with the planetary houses of seeds and pollen
to watch the river take on its serpent form
bringing forth an old sleep
from the bottom of things   things darkened
by a little light   heartbreakingly visceral
the luminous unseen threading through

meanwhile above me wasps enter and leave
their paper convent   Sisterhood of the Vespids
their contemplations severe
their shine leaning down into their dark eyes

other insects drifting about like ash-keys
wings hitched to whispers coming
from over the horizon
                          lifting them along
carrying them through the algebra
which we're always certain never adds up

I'll sit with arithmeticians in the moss
millipedes and the red-backed salamander
wait with them for the hour that comes eventually
to un-number things   to unthink the grand design
quietly as the sound of time settling into pearls
or paper pavilions unfolding just inside the mind

at moments like this I think of the Underworld
you seated there on your silver chair

all the walls stuffed with beards from the prophets
to keep in the sounds   all that longing
all those goodbyes beside the water

at moments like this I think of you
                              walking down to Acheron
your secrets crossing over   where the sign
beside the river reads *I flow with grief.*

A History of Sunlight

The Rouged Houses

all day the makers of edges have been cutting
into the emptiness from every side
making a life out of the invisible   a sad life
with sharp corners and children who the knives
rock to sleep each night in a drawer

the rouged houses I walk past in the evening
the white rooms and the apple-scented doors
enclose spirits distilled from sorrows
that only curtains could understand
only cabinets could possibly know

wives and husbands nod their heads in kitchens
brothers and sisters furrow their brows at tables
while babies cast the shadows of changelings
to the very margins of blankets wet with milk

after midnight when everyone's asleep in those houses
when the stars are upwind from the sun's absence
when the moon rises and it's a signal
for the slight things   for the silences to slip past
at the moment when the spider feels pity
at the moment you hear the hush of the catbrier vine
climbing upwards to the Promised Land never to return
then the premonitions come down upon those houses
rain down like pieces of burning paper

by then everyone is dreaming   murmuring with teeth
bared to a cutting edge and the undertalk all magnetism
attracting the stillness of cathedrals   of great halls

of auditoriums where emptiness is always felt so intensely
like an immense crowd pressing
                          into the centre of a violet
like a violet driven into very dense wood
like small blue axes and forests felled

and no sound in the falling.

A Hummingbird's Heart Beats
1260 Times A Minute

for Julia

This man will sit in his chair till sunrise. It's been a long day, and
now the conversations of the day separate the blades of grass to
lie down. Now the pauses between words possess everything. The
diligence of emptiness knowing no end that he can see, ecstasy of
blank spaces between the stones, and all thoughts out of the stones,
allowed to wander till morning. There's a sadness about him that
he can't interpret, like streamlets carrying strokes of blood back
to a source it doesn't understand. Like all the little sibyls under the
floorboards that can't speak a word, and the books on the shelves
that can't read themselves. In his room only the hummingbird
understands, pressed between the pages of the family bible in the
1850's, like a rose that understood flight, pushed flatly, woefully
against all the words of God. A flower where the darkness gathers
in the shape of a bird, where death gathers 1260 times a minute.
That's enough sorrow for even a man to understand, to find his
place, the weight of his unhappiness, that feather falling inside
himself, where there are no wings, no flying into light, not a
flutter, no answers coming from motion.

Ochre

the town consists of figures
painted on a cave wall in ochre
pictographs of a store   a few cars
a dozen or so people standing around

the lines have been worn by wind
and rain   patches are missing
from arms and legs
but the group doesn't seem to notice
carrying on with their conversations

someone has drawn a sun above them
so the day is warm and full of light
so the body is substituted for thought
as they comfort themselves
with the physical world

a stray dog will be added overnight
where the road dips down into attachment
where its back will touch sleep
keeping faith with the earth
its edges whispered into skin
outlines crying high in dreams
the match-heads of its claws
almost striking stone as it turns

some children will be scored out before sunrise
redrawn as parents waking to responsibilities
the sick will be washed   to fade slightly into the granite
a few of the elderly will be finally rubbed away
by the scurrying of insects across the surface of the drawing

tomorrow the sun will be erased with a gesture
rainclouds and a scrawl of wind will be added
so thought can return during the long afternoon
an aching behind the temples   desire
a force to collect the bits of colour that fall.

Three Ribbons

mother   the surface of the moon
is lit by the silence
of our small labours here on earth
the brushing of hair
folding of sheets   blowing
out of candles
all the energies it takes to light
a stone   a drifting stone
that part of an apparition
that always comes true

part of the ghost that is heaven
you and highest summer

mother I could remind you of how
the moonlight falls between the ferns
and the ocean
sitting on its haunches there
great beast of little height
biter of emptiness
upholder of two teeth
rattled with shadows

I could remind you that the world
is still here in deepest space
that the human heart is still
three ribbons tied to a belief
in flesh and form

I could ask now if death is loam
magnified to an absence

if the physical is the true
appearance of things
if the black-tipped eye
is where reality begins and ends

but mother I only ask that you recall
a moment in my childhood
as we stood watch in the grass
looking up at the moon one night
so that it was living and reaching
it was everything and nothing won
and how villages on the moon
rattled like plates as it rose
the villagers looking down
watched us so intently
that their selvages trembled,
and light fell from their eyes

I want to tell you to remind myself
of the last evening I saw you
as you drove away that province
was full   huge   low above the hills
and it looked as if you were
heading directly for it
and you were   ever so slowly
weakly   having only the energy left
to light a stone   the small labour
it took to follow a road

that night the moon was like a piece
of cloth bent at the corners

weighed down with burdens
sleep in one corner   death in another
the third held joy
in the fourth lay a shadow
shaped exactly like a child
a shadow thin as a veil
which shivered just a little
like three ribbons held in a breeze
which was dark movement   red movement
your fear of being alive.

Riding the Train in Secret

1.

the steel rails are almost hidden by the grass
and by weeds in the middle of their lessons
a schooling of sunlight next to the rusted drums
and cement blocks   warehouses that only appear
in dreams now   in tenderness

a train once rode these tracks twice a day
carrying people between towns that looked
exactly alike   that had identical names
and no one noticed that the people
who got off were the same people who got on

in the baggage car there were large trunks
and always inside some the merchandise of rewards
and always inside one that slight hesitation
used to decipher the movements of the heavens
and always death's thin bicycle leaning up
against the unlucky side of shadows
the white side that faces outward to eternity.

2.

as a child I rode the train with my mother
carried between the two versions of our lives
dogs escorted us along the tracks
then grew away from us   from our rocking motion
like birds being the parts of trees which grow
beyond the swaying of branches

my father never rode the train with us
never saw the other town   the other life

the journey full of tranquillity
a stillness trembling a little in its place
the kinetic movement of an endless whisper
that seam between leaving and returning
running down the middle of each thought

the train carried us through flights of spruce
and boulders that all looked the other way
ignoring our faces painted against the window
the way a dauber would have painted them
colours too fleshy   eyes too elementary

my father never knew of trains or windows
or of expeditions rolled-up in a child's chest
like illustrated maps of Erewhon
or the Valley of Gehenna   the blaze of outcries
rising from the soil   stretched upwards like grass

my father never travelled   never knew of roads
or of the slow passage into time
he lived with gut and needle
suturing anger to contempt to make an embrace
lifeless arms that fell like cloth to the floor
stitchings like crossfire
cutwork where the grief passed through.

3.

between the two towns the train slept
in its motions   dreamt of us
my mother and I talking softly to one another
speaking around the margins of our bodies
as plants do just inches from the light
the wheels rolled like scarves in water

the whistle blew at each crossing
a shriek of grey smoke   blowing
equatorial climates onto the surface of clouds
the brakes tightening and loosening
their one and only hold on reality

the town where we arrived was the same town we left
except my father didn't live there   never lived
or walked the streets with harm's custom
the accepted practice of removing warmth from language
all the names of the world that banks flesh from dread
all the words waiting their turn to be born

and when we arrived we would enter the house
house without the father
house in the shape of a bell without a clapper
bell with table and chairs   a kettle rustling
the water like dry leaves in a bowl

then the tea would be made with small gestures
like building a ship in a bottle   carefully
so the mast wouldn't break   so the taste
would find its way to our cups   gold-rimmed
red-breasted with a pattern of flushed violets

we would sip from our cups and I would feel older
than my mother and father   older than tea
that had the flavour of lost ages   of dank gardens
where stray boys slept when the earth was flat
before someone rolled it into a ball
so it would bounce back to us   all in colour

in bed at night I would still feel the sway
of the coach   and I would lie there thinking
and each thought was a division of light
till darkness came and I fell asleep among
the orphans of secrets who were never far away
imagining train rides like I did into heart's ease
a diesel running on hunger   the sound of swallowing
among the pistons   slight voices rising
from the wooden ties   the whisperers   the distances.

Childhood

every insect is a harbinger
                of what has just begun
the universe is held in small things
for safekeeping
                keeping safe the stillness
every silence is a lingering of absolutes
it's all the same god

every stone is a collection box
and whoever is worthy of silver
comes deep in the night to gather it up.

A History of Sunlight

1.

an orb spider hitches a strand to a branch
abacus of her viscera beading the movements

like me she's part of the rust and pulse
of the day falling and time only speaking
to the veiled face   to the whisperer
beneath the foliage   now wordless and still

speechless is one way for the weight
of the hibiscus to open   white against white
against light folding to half-light along the fence

speechless is one way for the traffic to run
down streets between the houses
pushing the inaccessible along a line of sight

cars pass with a sorrow shared between them
something lost when the motors were turned on
something like a promise to loneliness that was broken
loneliness of deep forests   old growths dark with genetic
drainage   everything that becomes lost
                                    when it flows into presence

presence is what I saw yesterday in the dead robin
extending its wings on a slow glide into the earth
beetles moving like fingernails along its back
a scratch but no itch   head bowed into a cold climate
ground-flying to Netherworld   to other private trees.

2.

the sky is shine corroding blue   clouds like seamounts
the neighbourhood softening to a fine dim silk
someone hitching it to a bough   someone weaving
the hours   one over the other   the highlights
and gloss braided along a hunger for infinity
and all that prettification cool against the skin

hours come and the gods keep busy in their corners
knitting chromosomes to disengagements   creating
pullouts of flesh and bone from apparitional dust
cut of the metaphysical   snip of the unknowable
signing everything in the low cuneiform of the self

sometimes the self peels away in late afternoon
moving off as the heat of the day collects on the faithful
on all those children playing madly in yards
all those flies with their snouts in the silk
those dogs running hard in their sleep
our lives wander off for a moment or an hour
and we never wish them back   it simply returns
simply enough like fetishes of absence
the shadowless idea of empty space
or the bodies of ghosts clinging
like damp newspapers to grass and to our wrists
as we reach for the car door   driving away
shredding numberless haunts of a physical world

I sit between the inner sides of my small landscape
by the roses   each a fortune-teller's table

a red fate   a white fate   stained by invocations
bees fly by with the strength of thumbs
crows fly by with the strength of hands
I sit unable to lift the hem of what surrounds me
Fate's diaphanous cloth of attitude and appearance
silks that breathe a transparence onto circumstance

I'm thinking of serenity's heartbeat carried on the breeze
just one beat   just once coming into what's to come

I think of Life pushing all of her heaven into spores
I think of Death walking behind us in the dark
his feet a swarm of hands picking up the distances
                                        lying on the floor.

3.

the planet pedals on slowly in the heat
while chlorophyll moves it closer to the sun
while along the sidewalk pigeons carry no messages
other than the universe cooing to itself in supplication
down the block children rehearse being human
good practice   multiple repetitions of joy and ache
summer changelings   each boasting up their holding
each standing like a curtain about to be drawn

the solitude of children   this is the way of heaven
it's the same for adults   this feeling of otherness
like a body within our body   like someone else's
fingerprints having easy passage through our skin
someone disremembering the intrigue of our hands
so we drop the water glass and the fall is luminous

and those dark panes on the ground offering a view
reminding us of what rushes into light
expecting birth and a grace and a world to appear
the accident   the shattered moment _ broken surfaces
all the small fractures in absence that brought us here

this is the way of heaven and I try not to forget
as two minuscule clouds drift by   almost motionless
carrying their single glass of water   afraid to spill it

this is the earth's signature   two clouds
and a damselfly gliding between them
till that almost imperceptible body fades on a mote
on a jot of the empyreal   little firmament   tuft of air

this is the way of heaven   that imperceptible fade
beating its wings to traverse the strategy of the self

the small self   that small silence lying to the night
                     saying it wakes when morning comes.

4.

the afternoon slants into further hours   jays repeat
the grand speeches of the gods and the missing word
wounds in the pine tree vein a light into the underworld
of the little songs   roots singing blades of grass
through their sequences   singing us to otherness

a ball of flames over Cancer and Leo   a crab and a lion
then a dog barking in the street   vertical to reason

a dog's sweep of visual perception   dog-sized   dog-born
the second sight of animals counting the suns we never see

there's so little we comprehend   yet we keep coming back
to the world   to sit under a star equal to locality
equal to the light on our skin   to the warmth in our blood
each thought and deed a history of sunlight
while Fortune draws straws   who will live   who will die
whose ache will be the ache of poppies
whose will be the pain of towns on fire
day after day and some of our lives shepherded through
sleeping on nourishment   eating the lower food
while night comes in both sexes   mating the inner world
to the outer   otherness to otherness
while a breeze moves hieroglyphically   symbol by symbol
one for God   one for God's absence
while the given is a heartbeat and a half-demise
half-life of a visitation among the weeds
while attendance comes
while the rain comes handing out darkness
                                    like books to be read.

The Star Bellatrix

the bride turns in a trance
red flowers fall out of her hands
endlessly into black space

her desire is a hesitance

her body warm as if she were dancing
spinning on a floor   her partner unbeheld.

Pearls

out in the dry grass of a grey day
the flies grow old and centreless
gradually drifting off to living rooms
to the screens of afternoon television

the family is packed in tight
against the soap opera
each face beautiful   glowing in the moth-light
each body slack and beyond communion
like the dead in the earth
with their symmetry poorly attended
making the gesture of pearls in a drawer.

Disposing of a Broken Clock

I put two final drops of oil in the mechanism
which is placing a word on either side of time

I anoint it twice   bless it in a proper manner
to pay homage to those cogs and gears
that held the hours in a drop of oil for so long
like dark wine that settled on an altarpiece
of moveable stirrups
                            coiled springs and mandibles

I carefully remove the screw that controlled
the weightlessness of the future and the one
that counterchecked the heaviness of the past

I wipe its face clean of hands and numbers
so it looks like the moon sighted through
longing   what the eyes have to endure

I remove the mainspring which shivers once
in my palm then is still   the stillness of harm
done   harm's way straining to be silent

finally at its centre I build a small campfire
to warm the ones who will come much later
those migrants   those small beasts who circle
us endlessly   who follow the ticking of the grass
and the straw that overtakes the wind
who know only an essential time lives on after us
who bow to the timepieces lowered onto their hearts
the continuum of water and the laze of stones.

A Petition to Clouds

for John Smith

along the borders of names and descriptions
a starling flies through her own network of nerves
with no means of escape   threading being
to nonbeing as we all do
our grave in our handshake   our death judging
the warmth of a kiss

all afternoon the rain has brought solitude to earth
almost soundless except for a trace of bells
along rooftops   more a subtraction of bells
more a fading from history of that knelling
that once placed time like coins on our eyes

the storm comes and the streets darken for God
the wind picks up the indistinguishable
and we are carried off through blades of grass
with no end to our journey

back and forth we go like spirits passing spirits
in an invocation   in someone else's petition to clouds

everyday we are almost here   come rain or shine
come illness or the resting place

from moment to moment this proximity to existence
can forget to speak and for an instant we complete ourselves
                                        in its stillness
our breath billowing out from under the soft burn
of stone on earth   that seam where we enter and exit the world
roots just beneath us   the sky just above us
each raindrop scratched by our nails as we try to hold on

to the memory of who we are   a namelessness soaked through
with transcendence   which preserves us despite everything
which is our dread   which is our consolation

our hearts perpetually beating against the end of things
tenuous fists pounding blood into the invisible
trying to give it life   trying to give the imperceptible a chance
and the rain falling with the names of everything
the rain falling with more secrets than we can hold.

Scratching the Back of Heaven

against the mountains and critique of clouds
the moonlight shines like ten thousand women
about to speak and the world half spoken to

sitting in the grass my memories creased
and folded into cranes   their flights
back and forth through unphysical lands

late September is a Japanese scroll appearing
and disappearing with each breath   Sumi ink
softly brushed along the river and remaining leaves

only memory scratches the back of Heaven
that itch between seeing and blindness
that real glint in the unreal

I'll wait beside the Bow River   the waters
sketched in freehand   remembering their
origins jacked from dust and old fires

I'll sit and wait for the black branches to come
for me   to lift me up one last time
to feel the memory of virga   the present moment
evaporating before it reaches the ground

the moon's calligraphers have begun their long text
someone's dream begins to putter about among the pines

meanwhile the ghosts of a few crickets are
                    sharpening their harps

meanwhile the golden frame of each star is coming
loose from its nail   sliding down to the horizon
twice fallen   body and light.

In the Province of Tharsis

your headlights breasting darkness
the rain coming down river mad

the road attending   present
at the turnings   at the stretches
that pass the fledge of woodlands
and farmhouses nailed together
                    with Braille
with all the blindness of effort

far above you the universe is silver
like hoarfrost heading south into the valley
like elegies written one after the other
aimlessly across a stagger in the blackness

your car keeps rhythm with a Paleozoic fire
brooded and cradled at its core
the combustion of swaths carrying you
wash of light off the couplings
                    and strains
scalds shredded into motion

the engine firing too early
pinging the air with weightless calls
cracks in the cylinder block
like hexagrams in the I Ching
As one goes, rain falls; then good
                    fortune comes

you are driving through wetlands
marshes where the swamp-broth
has starched to panes
and the skulls of ants grow cold
like signatures of stillness
written beneath the bracken

you might be anywhere   not just this world
holds you   not just gravity's asides whispering
carved spaces into your ear   places here
that can contain you   both feet to the ground

travelling towards your breath and west
to the dulse-coloured light at the horizon
you could be bucketing along on Mars
deep into the province of Tharsis
light of Phobos swaying in the mirror

or it could be earth with all its reality curbside
the towns   glistening woods   the ocean sipping
quietly at the grains of sand

driving alone on a dark planet with no destination
in mind   a stray becomes otherworldly
growing calm at the margins   wild at the eyes
deeper into the seeable than expected

the small agonies of the windshield wipers
their wet pules drawn across the glass

keeps you company   even the brakes asleep
in their ascendancy give some form of comfort
like the pavement beneath you hobbed
by tires and years of ice   pocks and scars
blowing off a bit of water when you pass
                              waking them to light

you have nowhere to go   so you go
smudge the road   trench the darkness
into passage   the slender trance of foot
and pedal moving you steadily along
to the next aftermath of shadows

to the rigour of absence at eye level

then on to that rope-burn at the skyline
healing to an illumination   to an abrasion
of all sorrow   and loss gathering there
sleeved at the horizon   like failed silks
all afire   tucking their ashes into time
into time's release and the dying light.

A Woman Watching

for Karen

1.

all morning you stand motionless
like a figure inside a box camera
blindfolded by a flash of light
standing in dark feathers up to your eyes
but not flying to escape

because you like the spring   rain falling on rain
the unborn coming to ask for mercy
but only trembling in unison like berries on a branch
only sighing a violet's small agony into the air
the light grows   the sky comes blue   comes to shim
the space between the stone's brood and the ant's temper
to be wedged in between the names of grass
and the fragrance of hills trampled down by crows

in fields serpents awake from deep sleep
with soil between their fingers
far out to sea turtles surface
like heavy doors that open onto stone
in offices people cover with slips of paper
the places where the bodies fell

you like the spring   viscera of ferocities
crawling up out of the ground   push of a bouquet
against the heart   snap of the universe
when it opens onto illusion   ether breathing in
the voices of cats and deer

you stand at your window   the tissue of trees
waving off the hours   the wind is an exaggeration
of both heaven and earth   the words that it brings
can't be pronounced   it is something about oblivion
something about birth   but more than that
something other than you or the landscape
or the rain collecting and its simmer upon your eyes.

2.

you surrender to morning   to worlds within worlds
to the rain's glide   scars of water on your window
each cluttered with the same thought that crowns each cell
memory of everything infolded   sealed in reflection

all winter you grew close to fading   diminishment held
a touch of relief   Braille of medicine in the night sky
stars embossed upon scattered ideas   raised dots along Greek myths
Orion coughing fires into blackness and blackness bowing in return
and you bowing down to wintry skies   a steady bend
beneath the wind's surge   snow doubting everything it covered
no evidence on earth to make it wonder   ever faithful to clouds

spring is the eye   sight destined to description   vision born
comforting the dead ends of things that are just beginning
joy's solitude at ground level   a bit of green holding up the heavens
fizzle of the ant in her egg   tailings of eelworms rusted clear
the stone's idle companions strewn to the horizon
the weight of here   the buoyancy of there
morning rising out of the dog's nudge   his bark across yarrow sticks
perseverance brings good fortune/pay heed to the providing of nourishment
and you are paying heed   watching the thresholds open up

for nourishment   the mouths of the dregs wide with anticipation
diligently fed by waterdrops and a trace of fire beyond the sun

yet you stare and are never certain of what you see
life is such a fading of positions   of emplacements imagined well
silhouetted pigments that the mind only knows in the past
shapes gone as soon as they're seen   you see them everywhere
dodged in gloss   mutable   heading off further into light
like a lens drawing Phoebus slowly to paper till it burns.

3.

the more you look the more things fade
it's like watching an eclipse
watching the horse drunk on its harness
drag a pearl across the sun

between the weather and your pane of glass
there is a legend told   how the world is silvered
to sleep by our watching   glimmered to dream
of our sight moving out over its inclusion
this is what it means to pay attention
all things falling into slumber when they are seen
a ghost is made to replace the ghost that's there
we walk away haunted by shadows
like the shadows of the sea
dry against the back of our hands

we must turn away to correct the deception
we must lose ground   shudder the trance
we close our eyes to wake the world.

In the Dream of the Silver Birches

All Our Wonder Unavenged

1.

particles of evening warm themselves in the afternoon sun
pieces of solitude gather slowly   one under each ginkgo leaf

I sit on a rock of saddlebacked granite
                                        I sit in a world of abundance
a handful of bees goes down to the river   two handfuls return
you deadhead the dog rose and two stray curs appear

you deadhead a memory and two more appear
longer and deeper and more alive than the last

I remember my mother seated at the kitchen window
her cat's-eye glasses staring out into the night
trying to find divinity and divinity's reasons

my mother believed God moved the sparrows around day after day
as a teenager I believed the sparrows moved God around
all the inexhaustible crutches He leaned upon
all the underweights of silence to find His way

now the only god I believe in are the sparrows themselves
                                        unaltered by my belief
their wings contain hollow bones where a pantheon could pass through
and they do   hundreds pass through at every moment
this is how they fly   by allowing passage to earth's beliefs
the little deities of the big thunder and the rain that falls.

2.

at my feet black ants run about   looking for a great storehouse
                    a little picnic   a little headhunting in the grass
they drink the dew and as far as I know curse nothing

I would like to curse nothing   to move about practicing quietism
perhaps find the great storehouse   do some headhunting
stick to a regime   the discipline of a feather falling
                                    from a sparrow's back
I would like to be called out and fall to the furthest limits of the finite
to a resting place among the relativity of all attributes
which would be home surely   where I began   where I no longer dwell
feeling time and space upon me now   a little dust in my eyes.

3.

a few clouds move in   riding the intersections of ancient thought
across the sky   old ideas that floated upward   Confucian dialogues
Sumerian rumours   prayers to Pallas Athena   Persian satires
Druidical ethics   not gone   not absorbed   not forgotten   just there
influencing us still   carrying our lighter burdens and the clouds

from where I sit clouds cast shadows on the flowerbeds
perennials along the fence that bloom like glossy photographs
of themselves   bright flowers stripped from shining pages
from catalogues that never mention the plant that doesn't exist
the imagined yarrow that the mind owns
                    that has neither root nor stalk   leaf nor flower

all my thoughts are a divination with yarrow-sticks
and a mere filament of flame   a single mouse hair burning
deep in a canyon   lighting up less than an inch of dead embers
the big fire   the full consciousness having moved on immediately
travelling constantly   never resting while in nature
while under Heaven's luminous regard.

4.

I've been seated here for three hours I think   difficult to be sure
without a watch or a column of diminishing sand
or a dog that scratches her head at ten minute intervals

time is a controversial work about which no one agrees
time's a bugger my grandmother said and she would know

time's a bugger and finitude a fluid state without a source

anyway time is passing for me and my piece of granite .
no point thinking about it   separating it out
Cling to unity the Taoists said over and over
till the nettles repeated it generation to generation
till you hear it on the breeze sweeping across fields and ditches

I'd rather contemplate nettles   follow their leaves
back to Culpepper's herbal   to the tonics of Hildegard of Bingen
I'd rather make nettle tea and drink to Lao-Tzu
but a shadow glides by and I have to look up

a bald eagle flies over   making his way down to the river
to fish the afternoon away   calendrical wing beats
time's wordless doctrine upheld and maintained
the wounds of salmon like minutes cradled in the hour's arms.

5.

late afternoon and the western sun-door still ajar
some hours to go before it closes   shadow hours
for the food gatherers to return to their mounds
for chickadees to follow their old ways
                                    fables without end

cosmologies of shadows gather up the light
                        from under hostas and azaleas
many stories to be joined into one before night comes

only one story after the sun slips over the horizon
                                    the one and the manifold
My face is the face of the Disk this is the deceased speaking from
The Egyptian Book of the Dead   from the other side of darkness
the bright side and its holy office trying to give us a hint
                                    an initiation into eternity
so we might find the eternal in perceptual experience

so we might find our way in the world   and the oncoming twilight
is the perfect time to find our way   so the Celts believed
that sacred in-between time   between worlds   betwixt night and day
when all crossings are possible   freeing us from duality
Dharma Path the Buddhists call it
Pollen Path of Beauty to quote the wisdom of the Navaho
and the bees would agree returning once more from the banks of the river.

6.

I sit on my rock watching dragonflies hover by
with their wings sheathed in calligraphy
listening to feral cats on the move
                    spreading their Tantric cries

while shadows grow taller and taller like adolescent boys

and dogs bark and dogs bark and I almost understand
their Indo-European tongues   their slang for sex   for death
their reasons for biting their masters   for venerating
the chase through the thickets   their unlimited awe
their wonder unavenged   all our wonder unavenged
all of it left hanging in the fetish-shine of the moment
a longing   a bit of animal-shine along our skin

they are nations the Koran says of the animals
and I believe it   a kinship of being and knowing
                              as deep as ours
as ancient as breath on the lips
and any meditation on this deepens our own being
humbles us before the cricket's leg and the badger's eye
and we should be humbled   fall to our knees

then comes stillness and listening
                              comes with kneeling
and listening is the language of the soil
                    Latin of the hawkweed
so I sit quietly without moving   while buried all around me
seeds lie on their sides   longing upwards to visible air
while dusk is falling   honeymooning the shadows
darkening the medicine   the metaphysics of the grass
while microbes repeat their silent mantras to themselves
soundless and drifting   all woebegone and woken
                    all Buddhas of Immeasurable Light.

7.

time to go indoors   drink from the glass
                                    eat from the plate
move the pages of a book around
or watch the news sway in its cradle of light

a few stars are up and Venus in her silks at the horizon
                            fresh from the underworld
a tracery of myths hammered onto her body
passing our lives night after night
where we all sit at a dark gate waiting for it to open
dreaming of lifting the latch of Morning Star
and stepping through to redemption

redemption is a dark game someone once said and muffled
I would add   like the whisperer inside the fox
calling to the whisperer inside the varying hare
                            a dark and distant game

too distant for me as I walk to the house

the moon is rising   cabbaging light from the weeds
full moon   full sides short of breath from the long climb

I walk and I could sleep in it   in the footsteps
in the motion given   jewel-give of the fireweed
scent-give of the lilies trying to keep all of summer down

I walk and birds are settling in for the evening
among the pine boughs   their small calls from tree to tree
like the voice of Proteus across his many forms.

A Lunar Hand Presses Spirit and Flesh

for Bobby

1.

the irises on the windowsill are blue   reason is blue
so that illness is the colour of a red theory fading among pinks
so that death is a colourless theory stubbed against black
so that nurses throw white before them everywhere they go.

2.

from your bed you can see doctors move and blur
hear porters carry all the proper sounds to their proper places

from your window you can watch the moon forthcoming
placing its stones into position above the harbour

from your room next to the dispensary
you can hear pills turn clockwise in their containers
orbiting suns too minuscule to see   like planets
in the dogwoods   following a star to its branch
a luminous branch high above a darkening river.

3.

you lie in bed bleeding into descriptions of fate
your death coming in a mottled ease
                          in an orderly moonlight
that covers your bed with the light of stones

death is when everything comes to know you at once
all at once   like the moonlight knows you now

a lunar hand under your bandages   just there

pressing together spirit and flesh till they are one
                                    or seem to be one
the required solitude at least for a passing
an aloneness allowing you to exist in the moment
the moment unchangeable   drifting beyond names
beyond narrative   something at the very end of things
what moves through the blue irises   what reason won't allow.

Ars Poetica

1.

a day slow and uneven like a dead rabbit
breathing from the other side
each blade of grass growing straight
                      as an actor's line
first green voice when the curtain is raised

no-see-ums seen circling   spudding turns
their bodies bound tightly as the gospels

a swallow flying through the insect surge
her every heartbeat pinching the air
             to see if she's still there

a few thousand alewives out in the bay
their lives one long shiver from beginning to end
a quickening of gnosis   a flash of blood

dogsharks at speed   all the cold-blooded en route

the sea's affection touching shore
each wave believing   always believing in that instant
that flash of time against land   the water striking
a continuance   a revelation inside itself
such a momentary awakening   such eyes in the collision
a view of the planet turning   such seeing in the dark.

2.

I walk along with words gargling flesh close to the bone
repeating things to my body that I would never say out loud

no shadows inside the body   that's what the mind's for
shadows and ghosts wandering about in neurohormones
the absolute blackened by the half-dark of language
each word biting the tail of the next
                            bestiary of the thin anthem
the one the self sings when no one is watching
a melody worded through with time remembering
the storyline   dark beginning   dark end

July equals time and dog days in the bloodstream
summer's instinct a long lament and hunt-down
of pillow talk among the leaf mould
sighs of the undone   blush of the assimilated

I walk on bruised ground   on God's awayness
the soil in tongues   preaching to the names of things

I walk along with a tobacco-coloured dog
his rubbery feet carrying the odour of that great horse
the one the Greeks built out of damp pegs and green wood
the black space inside that horse is his vocation   fated
for cathedrals but given to dogs   the vault of his heart
                            all that which was God so long ago.

3.

the Buddhists say the universe is a monastery
everything is a monk   galaxies   dogs   maggots
every mountain   every broken stem

black holes pulling our mantras into nirvana
insect calligraphers taking it all down   somewhere
under the fallen leaves and dross   given time
the Great Book will be written   but not by us

given time we might learn to read   but never scribble
a single sentence that will be weightless and endure

behind our backs words sign-off   return to the unwritten
the unspoken   to the stone's breath   to the steady absence
of what keeps us here   our lexicons fading across tips
                            of ragweed and groundsel
trying to hang on like spirits holding onto an altarpiece
wisps of expectancy   downspins in the dust
all the shadowless shadows we've put on the page
all the shapes sharpened by use and decay

a little haunting of ourselves in the small hours
with keyboard or pen   apparitional verso
or right-handed screen all aglow   with a poltergeist's
shine and a glance back at us over its shoulder

to write poetry is to sign-off the words yourself
take them from the visible and return them to the invisible
burnishing the backs of beetles as you go

to write is to enter the rehearsals of solitude
                              among the pine needles
shimmer there once or twice in what is already scripted
what is already in place and unnamable   alphabet
of black addressees   black house on the tip of a feather
on the hair of a dead rabbit breathing from the other side.

4.

the sun's fifteen-hour dream of us in the world
no rain for weeks   clouds short-sleeved in the summer air
jays with their Munch cries and their blue bibles opened
to blue covenants   Dionysus in the intestinal flora
of an earthworm   staggering   drunk on soil

overhead a crow's white heart at ease in its bridle
underfoot the hawkweed's security lights on all day

deer with coyote breath in their blood   foxes in wait
teeth darkening at scents rising from a half-pulse
under the hatching foliage   serpents hissing Morse
from their little heat   hawks bearing down

casualty and slaughter and no one a survivor
for thy sake we are being killed all the day long
my terrier barking with a lamb's force
                              against the low shadows

ley lines for night traffic   for moths and moonlight
brut wings and Mare Nubium dry as a pressed violet
only one path for walkers during the day
a curve around manifestation and back again to language

what takes me through this field takes me home eventually
to the blank page   cave mouth of the computer screen
Fingal's Cave hung with letters and the Three Conceits
better am I   equal am I   worse am I
a long spelunking to get past the Buddha and write anything
type in the diaphanous lines   tremulous in their disguise
like forgotten things half-remembered   widening into
silence and a melancholy almost readable

write and rewrite then shut off the light   roll the great stone
back into place   all flat land after that   all the way to sleep.

5.

Sunday and no ache for God among the hives
a late afternoon with a fetal glow at its edges
the field keeping its ear to the ground   listening to light
                                a world and a world away

nature's a heavy brocade to rest your cheek against
a rough green on a raised pattern   still it's all we have
that and its description   that and an endless monologue
we pour blood into from morning to night

blood loss cloistered into the plush of the infinite
birthstones of the small atrocities scattered
about at our feet   appraised once by Valentinians
                                precious in their glimmer

meanwhile the undergrowth shares a mouthful of air
spiders weave a translation of the Gitas from their silks
meanwhile a bear's dead weight in each drop of sunlight
three burning stars in each bead of darkness

reality fluid and incorporeal when we stare too long
at the strata of days   at the hours we never own

still we make do with a few syllables and a long journey
towards form and absence   a few wordless words
to melancholia   a few air kisses to the loose fittings
of an old narrative hard-bitten and unattended
                                        beneath our skin

still I walk beside my dog   walk this side of things
for now   this side of the rusted birches
where nature asks for our compliance in matters
of silence   in the unending measure of solitude
it takes from our stride each day

still Ekai's *Gateless Gate* seems wide open

still damselflies show up processional   preordained
Orphic in their wingspan   in Caravaggio reds and blues
which brighten the constant rearrangement of light
its fuse and mantle and its sleight-of-hand.

6.

evening now   Venus rising above the grammar
of crickets   July thaw of the full moon   bats
stretching out their fingers to flight   fireflies fluttering
quietly under the eaves of the dogwood trees

shining clockwise beneath monosyllabic branches
same word for each leaf   same name repeated
same result   green and endless and spoken for

soon we will go back the way we came   the path
already written   Brailled into the grass

for now we'll sit under the overhang of stars   while
all around us there's a partial bed-down of the spirit
sleep of thread and knot
                              to be untied later in the small hours

for now it's enough to sit and watch as a horned owl
glides across the ides of a dead pine   follow
the step-back of light into the horseweed   watch
wolf-ghosts walking like men   like the darkest ones

if you're motionless the stillness is broken in time
the blind-stitching of quietude showing through
small cry of a raccoon   like a baby locked in stone
squeals of deer mice running to the end of the story
the snap of a twig   stepped on by memory

from the yelp of a coyote it's a long walk home

from behind our backs   deep in the forest   a voice
has been laying itself down and picking itself up again
backwash of instinct and you'll know it's there
moving slowly towards syntax   making the sounds
of hunter and hunted   making language out of what
is seamless and inconsolable

this is the voice we hear above the page

this is the source of the shadows that fall there
one word   then another   then another

these are the footsteps of our master
coming home the long way   through worlds.

Black Straw

on the other side of the earth stars hive
in the celery pines   here the sun
is a liquid deletion of space
a melting of the present moment

noon   and time already gone
nothing but the laziness left to feed pigeons
and polish idleness to a gleam

I imagine far-off galaxies hold desire
as we hold an apple in our palm
here on earth apples and progeny help round off the edges
of pain   the sorrow and sorrows of consciousness

also flocks of sandpipers help us get by
and calico asters and the smell of sweetgrass
and I should add the invisible to that
the other world with its black straw
changing and contorting   taking their shapes from us
which is a comfort when we feel alone
with nothing else to support us but the ether

the earth is a hard place to imagine
if you had to start from scratch   start with apples
and build from there   or a single aster in infinite space
imagine a sandpiper sent forth from darkness
into darkness   returning with this warm afternoon
yet we see it everywhere   there is an aster in infinite space
there is returning   the apples build   there is black straw
turning into men   there is nothing else.

Campfire

when I make a campfire the forest learns
of my poverty   my penury here on earth
the match flares and it's like going home
after trying to find your place in the world
and failing miserably

I sit waiting for night   it nears through
the verge   down on all fours
and familiar with no one but God

it comes slowly through the trees
like a black dog turning its head from side to side
like a seeing-eye dog without its owner
still showing blindness a way through the world.

In the Afterforest

the moon is rising into her dream of alders
branches stained with keenings and pigments
that shutter   that move close to the possible

disguised as loss the rain falls and I settle
into the leaves   hunker into the bracings
of damp wood   dark as bedrooms where the
shadows of hands whisper fingers fast asleep

above me crows doze in slight rotations
of thought   dream the afterglow of their lives
the afterforest lit with their flights
afterwolves running below them
                    in streams of light

I sit with my tongue closed   my eyes blind
no address or longing   no name attending
only the hush of a single grassblade all around

seated with my stick   which is the old bed
I'll sleep upon when I'm dead   shaped like an hour
so a sharp end and a blunt end
I hold it in my arms   nesting by embrace
making it kin and friend   holding me in turns

deep in the forest   almost further than I can travel
someone is heartbeating a piece of silver
in her body   the birth will be painful
the child will be so full of the future
                    he will cry out for the past

for the books where he can listen to horses
passing through the Dipylon gate   to the creaking
of glaciers crossing the Rhine   to the invention
of fire and moving things

when I arrive there I'll be born   my mother
lying with tides of violets and blood
my afterbirth like a crow dreaming
feathering into the darkness
keeping faith with what I am.

Poppies

for Barney

cold sky   a December night in Nova Scotia
long-legged snow falling into empty flowerpots
Li Ho gone back into his book and closing the covers
easier to be warm in the spring of the late T'ang

the wind firm against handfuls of grass along the fence
where the bee's dead eyes turn to white smoke

trees and houses shake gently on their shelves
ice unleavened   flat against the ground
where the shadows of shadows smooth away

down the street a dog is barking madly
yet the silence is unentered by what happens

each bark is a red poppy bending under the weight
of teeth and jaw   it isn't a symbol or an emblem
of anything accessible or human
but stop to think of it and the flowered way will be lost.

Footsteps on Black Water

May blowing against the martyrdom
of the other side   against all the spirits
we've designed to carry us over   licensed
to lift us out of the body at the end

a few stars holding forth   pinned up high in the west
and the quarter moon airtight
                            like a jigsaw piece
fitted into the branches of a red pine

galaxies turning up there in the far corners
of an old ache   moving in circles
like fish crossing land   each sigh a world of dust
each song closed by singing

all night paradise drifts along as melancholia
on black water   it enters our hearts at 3 a.m.
it enters before we wake   before we begin
to make our daily pilgrimage to the door

not a word to guide us while in the world
no phrases to be séanced out of the ashes
of the delphiniums
no lettering across the unknown   no annotations
the apple trees stand unwritten in the orchard
their blossoms turn their pages and fall

nowhere for us to go   no journey   except
to follow our dark beginnings   pursue emptiness
mountains and cities placed across our path
dew scattered across exile like Pharaoh's wheat
and each horizon resplendent in its revelation
and each grave in the cemetery a child's grave
and every mother listens for us among the weeds.

The Silence of Remembered Time

1.

the town fathers are long dead
and with them the meditations
that were once their wives and children
and their dead dogs that resembled foxes
and their cats that resembled hares

the wharf has rotted and fallen into the sea
where spices and a second earth were unloaded
where brigantines and windjammers once docked
with figureheads of mermaids and Charlemagne
Artemis and Mohammed II Sultan of the Turks

even the theatre built for the future
out of rouge and gold foil
died the death of the inner faculties
first memory   then the stage
and finally the great chandelier falling
horrifically   deeply into the mind
now in that spot grows a Pleiades of trees
seven pines holding onto their shadows
like frock coats pulled in along their branches
waiting in the cold for the tragedienne to return
to brush the sorrow back into her hair.

2.

can you trace the figures of the townspeople
or even the transfigurings of their shapes
at night in their beds or along a stair
do you remember their footsteps   the rustle
of a certain dress against your words
human breath was turquoise then   greenish
blue and lifted softly off into the upper air
the human voice was that of birds
like pennywhistles far off in the trees
except for those whose jubilees lead them
to madness and the ravishment of hymns
their voices sounded like the entire world
returning suddenly from deepest space

can you remember their names pasted securely
behind their eyes on small slips of vellum
how they handed your smile back to you
with such elegant hands that it made you weak
can you remember their lips parted in tableau
their cheeks rounded by the mood of the calendar
do you recall their carriages light as suiting
or their roses that sang or the waltz that was lust

each died with the rain walking slowly ahead of them
up and down   along the grey esplanade
their spirits are souvenirs now   mementos
pendants of sentimental value   fobs of polished bone
adornments we wear at a slight distance from ourselves
remembering the age with a red spangle   or a plume
or a drop of pearls just there   at the back of our lives.

3.

what are we to believe of the dead   the paper sound
of their asides on winter nights isn't a proper sound
or their bones covered in flannel   stitched
with Christian threads from horizon to horizon
buried under candle stubs   those aren't proper bodies
those aren't proper smiles   black with entrancements
wide as windows opened to all the abysmal speeds
of decay and glory gone damp with sinuous shines
of Death's grease and rags and polish

the townspeople slid beneath the soil one by one
and their buildings followed them devotedly
carrying their belongings lamps   curtains
their postcards from Madras   their tea set from Siam
the change they left on the hall table   the pin
lost under the dresser   the plaster nymph offering
plaster grapes to a nutbrown Pan twisted round a tree
straining to change his position or his residence
they sank in time to the depths of the infinitesimal
to be reunited with their former masters
seated around elementary particles   sighing
like people do when dusk comes unexpectedly
when there are still so many things to do

what remains of the town are a few abandoned houses
blown through with weeds and the flicker of mice
rooms that fear the knock and the footstep
roofs that fear the cloud and the sparrow
these houses will soon join the others   they'll find

the streets they once knew nestled among
Death's juvenilia   his cobbles   his failed attempts
at paving the stands of moonlight along a crust of ether
his protracted experiments with crystals and asphalt
they'll find everything as it was before
except that future events will quicken the assignations
of the past   bring the heart swiftly back to the moment
that pierced it with an extinction   rising an utterance
so that dying will be considered speech   words spoken
a death of phrases at every turn   intones trenching
the emptiness between apparitional gestures
the stammer   the mumbling of claws upon a wrist.

4.

it's difficult being elemental at the end of the day
to stand in a theatre fallen among the subgross of atoms
to walk a stage with watery hands at your sides
unable to hold onto the dry edges of reality   unable to lift
the applause to your ear   the applause coming from nowhere
deafening in its equilibrium   the static balance of your name
thundering from all directions   dropped in another world
by those who remember you walking into a foyer or a garden
with your cape   with your lionheaded cane
that opened its jaws to roar at women passing out of sight
those who remember you with your blood beneath your skin

it's difficult sitting with the elements   to wear a coiffure
that wears a celestial point drawing you away from memory
to wear a tea gown covered in salacious weights   the obscene
affections and desires of the living patterned across yellow silk

the wilting of bows at the mention of sunlight falling on the pubis
the heat under your gown is a bear swelling upward like the sea
it's hairy like a sailor's back   it has endless beards like the sea

it's difficult so lie still   haunt the flyblown chronologies of the sheets
in your twelve-legged bed   be quiet and sleep past death   dream
of your house   with its walls laced with columbines and delphiniums
with vines moving under the flowered paper   like arms that might hold you
sit in your chair costumed in nightingales   enclothed in flight
the gramophone will speak in time   the perished words of the familiar
the silence of remembered time   take down the album without pictures
diary without words   silence is the paper blank   the papery instincts
of not existing in a tangible world   which gives the highest hope
so lie still and dream   the death of death will attend you there
flutter of space shivering warm beside your absence   the call to earth
the spectre undone by a birth   your birth full of glimmerings
a helping of flesh   a darkness that falls down bright among the living.

A Trace of Finches

for Margo

standing on a hill overlooking the Minas Basin
the sea calm   hidebound with moonlight
stars and throwaway galaxies swaying east
Minerva's bird gliding west on his mouse-run

quiet up here among the colourless wands of spruce
moths tracing thin bracelets in the air
fireflies drifting about with their gnomish-milliwatts
hives sighing in the undergrowth   a streamlet
crawling to Byzantium   its eyes down in the moss

below farmhouses have nosed in for the night
a fire behind each dream   a solitude behind each fire

an angel should appear just about now   to still the stillness
a divine messenger to pat down the hair of the sleepers

instead there's this bit of faith floating out there
somewhere above the valley floor   a wild belief
that the earth will sustain us   see us through
that we'll be angeled through with light at the end

I like the comfort in that   the small gods in that
gods small as finches   I think of finches
because when those birds all rise together into the air
it's like all the holy places
                         pulling away at once from the earth

I like the comfort of finches   a song's redemption
a feather's nudge into flight at the appropriate moment

what better wings to carry the soul away
a trace of finches drifting up Mammon's outline
to be elegy-plated high across the grief of the world

a long grief finally at truce with our senses
a flutter of plumage and an avian resolve

the way opened to a lingering darkness
a wayward shine from the receding light
the way small birds arrive and take our breath away.

The Field Sadness

clouds known by heart and sunlight weighted
                              down in the west
silence beginning to dog the songs of the cicadas

all saints are whisperers   especially here in the grass
prayers and the field sadness quietly mentioned
then a nod from somewhere beyond the trees

a few hundred crickets walking about   half-dreamt
woolgathered from an immeasurable grace
a few mice un-souled each day   unedged in eternity
the past tense of rain assembling the divine
water reflected in water and angeled to a blackness

between the stones where I sit   in the niches
there are endless paths that can lead you home
but only one small breath to take you there
the ant's breath golden between heaven and earth

a home in the wound of things   along the places
where the blood has dried   where we can set up house
and open red blinds to let in the sun

high above that house the grass sways like dark fish
windows open like the mouths of children
and doors ground down the final ache of the day

overhead an ontology scratched on insect wings
carries the consequences we've turned away

deer come forth   inseparable from the breeze
their essence like dew collecting on water

all around us cats still hunt down the Pharaohs
the memory of lost kingdoms tightened
throughout their bodies in synaptic shine

around our house the drear and drift of dying things
to sing us to sleep each night like latches released
one by one   to open our own death wide in the echo

we close our eyes and dreams of the world unravel
like benedictions caught on a high branch
like sorrel blossoms bending forward to untie their yellow hair.

In the Dream of the Yellow Birches

for Barry

Heaven is inscrutable,
Earth keeps its secrets
~ *Li Ho*

1.

the sun's yellow throat at the horizon
the thunder keeping in touch
rain falling in choirs

I come inside to make tea and read
from *Poems of the Late T'ang*
to feel all those lost moments
resurrected in this afterlife
to feel the dead move slowly
like honey turning over in its comb.

2.

pages slough off their words   remain blank
for a few moments when the cover is finally closed
when it opens out to a great distance

the reader also sheds what has been written
what remains is the light twice removed
from paper   essence of a weightless and thermal rise
of blood
layering in where the words lost their way.

3.

constellations rising above clouds and houses
sidereal enzymes drifting through the streets
one barking dog giving us a distraction from the zodiac
so add one more mutt to paradise   one more set of teeth
to bite down on perdition

also add this pseudoscorpion crawling across the wall
a minuscule piece of architecture from the *Book of Revelations*
now standing perfectly still   a perfect word in its chest
for its next move across the abyss.

4.

the night four hours old   rain gone out to sea
God already sealing the lips of the sleepers with fire
angels already taking on the form of our ill effects
demi-present and yet bright in our dreams

hard to see the Mycenaean grave of each rose in the dark
each place where the colour of grace is buried
along with the first voice of the invisible

hard to see the inlay of ghosts in the spider's web
or sense the sleepers shining back from the other side
the sleep of others buoys up my hand and these hours
also this book-scorpion finally beginning its blush
                          and journey once again.

5.

spider-optics checking me at the backdoor   black into black
the fingerboards of its legs spasm slightly in the silk
eight eyes on its face   two turned inward watching the silence
of the self   the self we share   shadow-crossed in the same
                                                            shadow

out there earwigs and cutworms filing down the begonias
a cat sleeping it off   the dead combing the yard's dark hair

a fine mist stretched out above the mulberry tree
holding its breath   living through its own disappearance
as we all do   fadeout to absolution on the far side of belief.

6.

some breaks in the clouds revealing pieces of radiance
an extragalactic nebula or two above the mini-mall
a few autos-da-fé burning bright over cars of the heretics
soon the traffic will die   the earth will go still
stilled and brought to its weight on an azalea leaf

we live in a storyline on a spinning world   no escape
flash forward then back   flame up and out like a match
struck hard once against a wall   a pinch of fire
autobiographical fizzle   once and we go out.

7.

when Heaven breathes out Hell breathes in
between breaths we write down the word *river*
and are carried along
we scribble the word *healing* on a wound
and place it in the current   but only once

tonight rebel yells   squealing tires
police sirens   ambulance sirens
all sailing by on a bottomless drop of water

tonight the celestial mandate is still upheld
so time shines forth from the undergrowth
so in the grass obscurity is indistinct from fame

later I will read what Solitude has written on
discarded boards   on the underside of stones
I will read the ten thousand chapters of the leaf's
fall to the earth.

8.

the clouds are drifting west to east   prayer smoke
carrying our sorrows and lamentations far from the city
two hundred chapters or so floating above us
unreadable and votive like the sky itself

up there it's still the third century BC   nothing has changed
the same doctrine looking back at us as the Taoists attended
the image of the imageless   unceasingly it continues

down here the backyard holds onto its medieval light
down here blood finds the rose   red finds its mate
and a feral destiny follows us through to the end.

9.

bats glide by on the receding warmth of time
clouds brush away the clouds
more stars appear   stigmata bleeding infinity
                                    into darkness

also a few nighthawks on pilgrimage   an owl
perched high on someone's afterlife   a housefly
dying a straw death   small spins and weak buzz
nerve endings unplugging
                        from night's diminished returns

a few rosebuds tonsured by aphids lean back
in their seats   a few skeletal weeds lean forward

such things that signed onto mortality
to an offer of weightlessness after the candles
are blown out   after the flames dampen down to ash

bone and flesh build the world in their own good sleep
build around a stillness always a lifetime away

we rise from the same place as the place itself
but half-lit by half-things shining off the guise

the moon has risen   the waxing part   sickle
in the lifeline   blood pouring out as darkness
all the way down to cars and 4x4s parked
and laid bare   waiting at the curb patiently
for the seen to be unseen
for the End Times and a long walk home.

10.

July's bloodlines flow to an inner alchemy
apparitional and encrypted in our bodies
secret messages from old destinations
old silences of someone else's heart

dark hours feeding us from pursed lips
their tongues nudge ours and we swoon
like clouds touching pine trees   like
gardens moving out over water

we're given what will sustain us
a few fingerprints on the moonlight
one or two monks behind our backs
tending to quietude

some hieroglyphs afloat in the low places
filled with water   mosquito wings   bits of grass
hair   flakes of skin   which predicted our lives
our every word and gesture   every thought
preordained and written down in a hieratic form
of dross   outtakes of the fallen   fallen and
                                        undeciphered

we're summoned and held by what we never see
according to the teachings of the Masters
all our kingdoms lie skin deep on the ground
erased by our eyelids closing in prayer
or by any whisper from any promised land.

11.

these night hours shapeless and moving
like tenderness along a sword's edge
before it is raised   like the passion
of the dog violet before it is seen

these hours waiting for us to cross over
to stumble in   trip over the martyrdom
of our first life and fall into our second
transformed and fearful   confluence
of semblance   bloodlines and ashes

frightening to accept it   dungeon-work
that inner life bound in darkness
                              by an intense grace

bound and held   small bead on a thin strand
carelessly hung between heaven and earth
somewhere out there above the milk vetch
above the fires twice born in the hive

not much security in that   not much camouflage
yet I find myself in God's sleep again and again
in the dream of the silver birches
                              taking root in the soil

yet I find myself witless and godless
constantly testing the air and water
for any little absolute anxious on our behalf

insecure and silent are the ways of the self
one life for another   one cloud for another
white chapters adrift   unreadable and votive

I try to follow Meister Eckhart's advice
Do exactly what you would do if you felt
most secure   sometimes it takes
sometimes it doesn't   meanwhile saints
graze on the begonias   meanwhile
ravens go to the edges of the earth
and return with our hearts in their beaks

the ones we thought were in our bodies
the ones we thought were redeemed.

NOTES

Leaning On Silk:
writ on water. From John Keats's Epitaph for himself: "Here lies one whose name was writ on water."

Twa Corbies:
"Twa Corbies" (Two Crows) is an anonymous poem in the lowland Scots dialect, possibly from the 14th century.

The the comes from "The Man on the Dump" by Wallace Stevens. "When was it one first heard of the truth? The the."

Walking Down to Acheron:
I flow with grief. Acheron, from the Greek αχος ρεω, "I flow with grief."

Riding the Train in Secret:
Erewhon. Erewhon is a fictitious land described in the novel *Erewhon* by Samuel Butler.

A Woman Watching:
perseverance brings good fortune/pay heed to the providing of nourishment. From the *I Ching*, 27. I / Corners of the Mouth (Providing Nourishment).

In the Province of Tharsis:
As one goes, rain falls; then good fortune comes. I Ching, 38. K'uei (Opposition).

Tharsis. Tharsis is located on Mars's equator, at the western end of Valles Marineris.

Phobos. Phobos is the larger and innermost of Mars's two moons.

All Our Wonder Unavenged:
Proteus. In Greek mythology, a prophetic divinity. He could change himself into any shape he chose, but if he were seized and held, he would assume his usual form of an old man and foretell the future.

Ars Poetica:
for thy sake we are being killed all the day long. From Romans 8:32-36 "For Thy sake we are being killed all the day long; we are regarded as sheep to be slaughtered."

better am I   equal am I   worse am I. The "Three Conceits" from the *Dhammapada*, a collection of the Buddha's sayings, probably compiled in the 3rd century B.C.

Valentinians were a branch of Gnosticism.

Ekai's Gateless Gate refers to *The Gateless Gate*, a collection of koans, recorded by Master Ekai, also known as Mumon, who lived from 1183 to 1260 in China.

Mare Nubium, "Sea of Clouds", is in the Nubium basin on the moon's near side.

ley lines are believed by some to be alignments between stone circles, ancient holy sites, etc., that contain power or energy.

In the Dream of the Yellow Birches:
Poems of the Late T'ang. A collection of Chinese poetry from the eighth and ninth centuries A.D., translated by A. C. Graham.

the image of the imageless   unceasingly it continues. From the *Tao Te Ching*, Chapter 14.

Acknowledgements

I would like to thank the Canada Council for their continuing support.

Some of these poems were first read at the XI Festival Internacional de Poesia de Rosario, in Argentina. I would like to thank the Arts and Cultural Industries Promotion Division (ACA), Department of Foreign Affairs and International Trade and the Canada Council for the financial aid which allowed me to accept the invitation.

The poem "All Our Wonder Unavenged" was first published by The Institute for Coastal Research in March 2006, as part of the Ralph Gustafson Distinguished Poets Lecture Series. The chapbook titled *Poetry and the Sacred*, was a result of a lecture given at Malaspina University-College in October 2005 while I held the Ralph Gustafson Poetry Chair.
The poem, with my drawings, was also published as a chapbook by JackPine Press in September 2006. With deep thanks to Barbara Klar and Jennifer Still for all their help and guidance.

Thanks also to the editors of the following magazines where some of these poems first appeared:
Grain
Poetry Wales
Saturday Night
Signal Magazine
The Fiddlehead

Don Domanski was born and raised on Cape Breton Island and now lives in Halifax, Nova Scotia. He has published seven books of poetry. Two of his books (*Wolf Ladder,* Coach House, 1991 and *Stations of the Left Hand,* Coach House, 1994) were short-listed for the Governor General's Award for Poetry. In 1999 he won the Canadian Literary Award for Poetry. Published and reviewed internationally, his work has been translated into Czechoslovakian, Portuguese, and Spanish.